CURDLED SKULLS

Selected Poems of BERNARD BADOR

Translated by the author with Clayton Eshleman

Black Widow Press is an imprint of Commonwealth Books, Inc., Boston, MA. Distributed to the trade by NBN (National Book Network) throughout North America, Canada, and the U.K. All Black Widow Press books are printed on acid-free paper, and glued into bindings. Black Widow Press and its logo are registered trademarks of Commonwealth Books, Inc.

Joseph S. Phillips and Susan J. Wood, Ph.D, Publishers
www.blackwidowpress.com

Cover Design: Kerrie Kemperman
Typesetting: Kerrie Kemperman
Collage cover art: *Recycle* by Bernard Bador

ISBN-13: 978-0-9842640-9-4

Printed in the United States

10 9 8 7 6 5 4 3 2 1

CURDLED SKULLS

Selected Poems of BERNARD BADOR

Translated by the author with Clayton Eshleman

ACKNOWLEDGMENTS

Some of these poems appeared in the following magazines and blogs: *Kayak, Poetry LA, Sulfur, L.A. Weekly, Conjunctions, The Jivin' Ladybug, House Organ,* and ActionNow blog.

Some of these poems originally appeared in *Sea Urchin Harakiri,* Panjandrum Press, LA, 1986. That book was funded in part by a grant from the National Endowment for the Arts, Literature Program.

Many of the poems, in their French originals, were published by Editions Saint-Germain-des-Près, Paris, 1977, 1980, and 1984.

CONTENTS

CURDLED SKULLS

APPENDIX

TRANSLATOR/EDITOR'S NOTE

I think that it was in the beginning of 1980 that the poet and collagist Bernard Bador called me in Los Angeles, where we were both living at the time, and asked me if I would consider translating some of his poems written in French and published by Editions Saint-German-des-Pres in Paris. At this time, Bernard was working as a Vice President of the Truflex Rubber Company in downtown Los Angeles. We got together and over the next several years translated several hundred of his poems; forty-four of which were published, with some of the originals, by Panjandrum Press as *Sea Urchin Harakiri* in 1986, with my introduction and a postface by Robert Kelly. Panjandrum folded in the 1990s, and the book has been out of print for over a decade.

After Joe Phillips at Black Widow Press last year expressed interest in Bador's poetry, I asked Bernard, now living in a restored winemaking building in the Beaujolais countryside, to send me some new poems that I could add to the translations published in *Sea Urchin Harakiri* for a new collection to be entitled *Curled Skulls*. He sent me around seventy poems, all undated, and I immediately noticed on reading through them that some were alternative versions to poems I had translated for *Sea Urchin Harakiri*. Most of the poems were in French with Bernard's sketchy literal English drafts, and some of these drafts lacked their French originals. I chose what I thought were the thirty most engaging pieces and either finished the translations or, in the case of the poems in English drafts only, edited them into their present form.

For the present collection, Black Widow has decided to print only the English translations. *Curdled Skulls* thus includes the forty-four poems from *Sea Urchin Harakiri*, the thirty "new" pieces in a section called "Curdled Skulls," and my original 1982 introduction along with Robert Kelly's 1980 postface, both of which are now presented as appendices. Besides being a unique poet, Bernard Bador is also an extraordinary collagist (as I write this note, he is packing up collages for a retrospective exhibition in Shanghai this November). One of Bernard's collages graces the cover of this book.

Clayton Eshleman
Ypsilanti, September 2009

SEA URCHIN HARAKIRI

OUTLAW

The dice
of dawn
have been thrown
over
the mountains
of genitals
subjected to
impeccable rape
by perfect Nazis
in a field of barbed wire.

Watchtowers
guard
the slaughtered
ads
of captive forests
marching
toward hampers
of the soiled underwear
of oppressed hours
of emaciated turds.

Cemeteries
of beds
float
in the icy pallor
like carbonized oceans
hanged
from the rusted
hooks of butchers in their Sunday best
for the feast
of the hordes of epileptic invaders.

Under
the sickly
lamps
the infinite procession of the dead
carrying the living
like rats at arm's length
toward the plastified formulas
of astrologers in cages
barred
with the automatic masks
of departed queens
bearers
of empires
for turtles in revolt.

DEATH OF A WORLD

The wind agitates
the iron cages
suspended
from gigantic bitter roses
of wakes
of blades of blood
pursuing
the first sunsets
before the music
of moon fires.

The mirror remains silent
on the gazes
drawn and quartered
between the enraged hoofs
of ageless stallions
of quaking ice
veined
with explosions erupting
at the surface
of slag
alphabets.

Fallow gods
have swallowed
the glass of swells
of birds
at the frontier
of the anti-smoothed plumes of silence,
listlessly
adrift
blue mescaline
expansions.

The genitals carved
in tepid fountains
parch
the she-wolves
of algebraic tribes
at the superhuman peak
of chasms of stems
between the muscular eddies
of phlegmatic
flesh.

ESSENCE

In the frondescence
of waking
blued by secret meathooks
sleep
holds vigil over lightning
spiraling between platinum naves.

Cripples
toss and turn
in the quicksand
off stage
where inert pulsations
are read upside down.

At the detour of alerts
shouted on the sickly
orbit
of fleeing upheavals
origin
ends.

THE SEA

Frightened crabs
scythe the wobbly forests of Ursa Major,
their claws fracture
the guffaws of nautical frescoes.

Soft antlers of spume
shred elegantly
against the surf of railways.

Perfidious, the anemones suck in,
ever so gently,
the nerves of nesting lagoons.

Passers-by
hurrying toward suicidal time
succumb to horny medusas.

The sea,
uncompleted earth,
rolls the ash ambergris of human spasms.

THE TRANSPARENT MAN

In the recessed tomb of eyelids,
the recumbent statue honks the crucified's horn.

The eyes deflate, saturated with beaks
concretized by the cold.

Inside the cage, space pleats, unfurls,
then shreds under the claws of roots.

Before your very eyes the sky swells expanding
gigantically to swallow the Niagara of the dead.

"THE GREEN QUEEN"

for Pierre Henry

Gravity of the voyage
in the well of itself
blocked
at the confluence without Messiah.

For every peacock
there are cymbals
at full tilt
on the rotted bridge of a disemboweled pubis.

In filagree
on the skin of the masquerade
the crackling of jujus nibbled
by horn-hard copper crickets.

At the rebound of the mouth,
a rain of pebbles patters
moss chokings
on the creaking door of garlanded smoke.

CHECKED

The wind pierces the horizon of the dead
between your much too white hands,
the snow is agonizing.

Night, taken by surprise,
escapes belling
through the handcuffed eyes of the grillwork.

Barbed wire entanglements of fog
are lacerating the scythed suns
with predatory shipwrecks.

Fake grand masters
are building empty cathedrals
for the death dances of gaping rose windows.

Under your battered eyes
in abandoned quarries
the blood of reasons coagulates.

SPLEEN

The weight of the world
hanging from a dead leaf.
All the winter bamboo
bent under the world's grief.

SUICIDE

A dream of razor-striped butterflies.
Bolts from lightning houses
at the tips of bladed waves.

Behind gardens of sand
a fossilized sphinx is cursing the Sirens.
The sun has slashed its veins.

EVIL PORT

Night disembowels itself on the rocks,
a hideous wrackish mud is filling your mouth,
the sand is choking in your heart of hearts.

All has fled—except the soul slag
dangling from the gluey harbor's crane,
mist of visages in dry-dock, beakful of bearded owls.

STRUGGLES

The slime suffocates in the grip of strangler
moons. The sea's moving blue immobilizes

fleeing reflections. The sand, with shiver
clubs, propagates concentration camp

migrations. On the reefs, branchy
cormorants shred the night's hypnosis.

CANCER DREAMS

Dryness of nothing, ricocheting
from tumultous thuds, bursting
against high liana drums.

Deafening greens of suns, of mud.
Light off greasy soup
scarfed by scorched flies.

Toads who cannot even remember
to remember are waiting for a caravan.

In the spreading river of setting sun
guillotines' ponderous thirst.

SABOTAGE

for Céline

Under tons
of putrid laundry
the pitiful plane trees
sag.

In the evening
salad greens sweat
the urine of consumptives
wandering about drunk.

Shreds of corrugated iron
heavily and stalely perspire
a rancor grown rancid
under the spoils.

In their purulent dreams
the slum kids
suck
on rat tails.

On the vomit giving birth
the asphyxiated air
of drunken cries
peels its scurf.

Ceaselessly,
sirens
sabotage
the freshly-sown suicides.

"JOURNEY TO THE END OF NIGHT"

Man gnaws his eyes, his blood and his bowels
before a tiny pile of fat, eczematous
pennies which pustulate in his hide of
a goatskin bag tanned with gold.

A bronze liberty kicks him in the ass,
blows of terrible hunger satiated
in garbage cans where the light itself
is rotting. And his dreams give off

rancidity like gravel buttered on thick
slices of bread in the harbor of dragging
fog on the mutilated sea of prosperous
cargos. The acne of mobs, disemployed

from life, suppurates on the stars of
washed-out decals of a sealed mass grave.
A cosmic anal filth corruscates
hemorrhoidal light on the rubble orbit

of copulating vermin. And the sun,
too handsome to soil himself in this miasma,
unloads his lead clots into sewers
overflowing with the aborted.

To hell with these scrap soul
merchants, these hucksters of blood!
But the nerves are already forging
their calvary in the future ghettos.

THE JUDGMENT

Harpoon
which pierces only showers of soot

and then, tarantula matches
in the gaping pit
of spelling-books in syrup.

You want to write a saga
on the royal love-making
of tigers in melting snow

and your last eye
falls, vitrified,
into the septic tank.

The wriggling of lights,
venom of colors,
attracts the larvae, tide of drooling.

Distress
of plastic Solanaceae.

THE HAND

A wall of flies
advances across the pulpy sores
of gravediggers
on a pilgrimage to the sources.

On the altar,
where the bones are smoldering,
a hand gloved in gold
paws the Cabalistic dust
in order to strangle the numbers.

MOMENTARY TRUTHS

Russett osprey scannings
mated in the ivory of a limpid
mirror. Through the blue
fissures of solar wounds,
a suddenly soaring eagle.
A spring tide from bites
precisely at the shadow eater's
lapidary leap. In playing-card
garden, a dial of quarter-hours
imprisons the endless
childhood jigsaw patience.

ARCHEOLOGY

Cuneiform quadriga lift up sand-entombed
arches of the sky's high fractures.

Inscriptions—like bizarre gardens—
burgeon in the shadow of eclipses.

Ablutions of history, the crumbly pottery
of granaries disemboweled of illusions.

The somber march of ancient statues
forces a passage for vessels. Beyond

the peaceful feluccas, mythological
glories have rejoined the primal silica.

SURF

Perched on the crest of the surf of light
man weds the frail tangent of the divine
ellipse. The sea slides on
itself, then recedes from the delirious

calling of the sun. A torrent of abyssal
stars bears transient kingdoms toward
the falls of silence. God has,
in this immense fluid belly where orgasms

agonize, condemned his own birth.
The undertow drags its shadow where
volcanos, covered with lotus caskets,
slumber. Dolphin guardians of the Temple

dance ritual calligraphies before "death by
signs." The approach passes
on the salt of the desiccate word,
dust fine as light

constellates the concierges' absurd broom.

DESTINY

Why do you run among the brambles of migratory birds
toward equators copulating with passers-by
for wars beyond pendulum-regular matador time
flinging banderillas into the keen cells of blinded arenas?

Stone bubbles are bursting on the piano buried
under coca cans, carnivorous flowers from acidic lands
where dwarfs prosper flattened against garish shopsigns.

At the flea market of light years, you'll find,
for nothing, many empty treasures of the Aztecs of tomorrow,
their hearts torn out by knives of moon spirals
at the baying of the musketoons.

Dozing Buddhas inhale luminous rays
in the hollows of tender lobes stretched
listening intently to lotus clouds
drowning in the old blood of shattered frontiers.

Don't you hear the planet drums
on their way toward nomadic ellipses?

Transhumanic silence follows
the sovereign tides of scenery lying fallow.

Again the universe falls—
unending cascades at the foot of the phantom bird
carved into the foam of secret sails lacerated
under the furious gallop of hordes of wooden horses.

In the distance a caterpillar
nibbles the fireworks at the horizon of parallel
berserk ice floes along the thread of maddened
blades toward the flaming magnet of universal
meetings at the points of pins.

THE FISHERMAN

goes out to cast for time at the end of silent
magnetic striations. Between the stillborn

waters of never to be gratified circles the line
snapped. Slow fishes of lures are again swimming

the fixed hours of perpetual motion. Under forests of
invisible executioners, they are whispering to

springheads about the mysteries of dead cells.
The mass floats, sterile, empty, the stars have fled

over the railroads toward conscious caverns.
Matter slips in through the fisherman's senses.

He has snagged the universe and, suspended in
reincarnation at the end of his snapped line, smiles.

ODYSSEY

to Saint-John Perse

A powerful sea of lemons
is lifting
over the firing-squads
green clouds
of empty thrones.

Your lips tumefied
with incense bites swell
at the blast of hunting horns
in deconsecrated churches'
luminous coal.

Don't you hear
the burned forests being hunted down
on the forbidden trails
of the exoduses
of your cemetery-tied hands?

With pubis blows
set in a cloud of fever
one must fell
the perfumed lianas
of black religions.

Suddenly
the corsair's keel
crashes into the carcass
of drums abandoned
in the cannon-enclosed wind.

At precisely the foam of lies
I will nail up
the exasperated
tunnel sun
in which you lie in agony.

Have you not seen the legions of angels
falling
like beribboned locusts
over the pyramids of alphabets
as they drift toward Cygnus?

On every side
of the soft octopi
marching toward echoing depths
ramparts check
the droughts' assault.

In flabby silences
that absence alone troubles
every voice
skewered by lunar blades
shreds.

Higher
the sacrificed gaze of the goldsmith
has polished
the insane battle-
encrusted mirror.

In the snow of calendars
buried
under gentians
the chamois-
yellow vessel has sunk.

The thirst of fetishes
carved
into the curare of anguish
are choking
in thick African furs.

In your flesh of steppes
let the nomad
sculpt the amphore
into which cavalcades of powerful
four-in-hands are poured.

Under the reign of huge rose windows
submit yourself
to the invasions of gargoyles brocaded
with the flags of pungent winds
from Bactriane.

On the backside of druidic mistletoe
contemplate
the milky armfuls
of meditations
of soaring rock forests.

On your jet-black hair
vast migrations of hours
are spreading over
the brilliance of royal favors
on the tattoos of slaves.

Caravans
move out
in the blue rose of dawn
toward saffron landscapes beyond
the gypsum found in fathomless eagles' throats.

After the exile of the ants
you follow
the putrid hyena flesh
as far as the pestilence
in which shadows graze.

Don't you hear
the dance of grimaces
on the bare walls of your fears
sacrifice your pride
to the waking of menhirs?

A gigantic avalanche of silence
crushes
space into a fleeing expansion
of blue atoms, hard and cold
stellar seeds.

APOCALYPSE

Madmen plunge their rage into a sweat of tears
while plundered temples cast out their mummies
into the ignorance of winter.

Masks of sawdust dance between the white bamboo
at "the festival of fear"
to the bone-chilling airs of the denied tundra.

On the edge of equilibrium
the strange veers its weather vane, a space
taboo, where frost banners are flapping.

The moon's wire meshes have hooked
the heavy feathers of disappeared springheads to
the deaf drums of grey rocks.

Night slices the blood of turtles stampeded
through the swift funnels of icy dawns.

Exposed to the wind under flags set out for jousts
without ladies
steeds surge down upon the stiffened buffoons.

A rebellious marine sun has encircled
the lifeless standard of the harvested phoenix
in the quicksilver of ossuaries.

BIRTH

Camels pregnant
with flies searching for facetted
fissures.

O forger wells
of bones gone to seed!

High priests
initiated into impotency
pack up the graffiti of C.O.D.
liturgies.

Better to make a hole in the air
than at a blind intersection
to core the bulbs of the Cross.

Acrid,
a spar of rose wreckage skims the second,
a wound of light
on the faded mandala of eyes in ashes.

Behind all this,
a long mauve cry is escaping,
its high note has sliced the petrified biruti.

Stillborn, flies
are swarming
the skin of veiled Vestals.

Soul
hookable
wall.

PROGRESS

Jacaranda blindings
heightened by summer's ponderous cymbals.

The melody slinks off to die
under a rolling-mill of potato bugs,
ardent myosoti spouses.

Under the flashings,
faceless sucklings
are flaying the dancers.

The turbulent macaw mutism
is quartered on a wheel of main-jibs
swollen with bear bites.

Tristan Tzara tramples the sacred wells
of the peacock butterflies
scythed by shamrock machetes.

At the call of the termite totems,
pastel blue moray eels
begin to lay tides,
popping sleigh-bells
under the murmuring of heraldic sables.

Ah charisma of deluges!
Hand-to-hand of turgescent mud
into which asphyxiated
walruses are plunging their tusks.

ANABASIS

Leather nights are galloping in the field of faces
O whips of screams
on thundering rumps!
By sweat sowings the poppy crowns the sky.

A vast frost of prayers
is admiring itself in the echo of crevices,
bronze and marble stallions
are charging the wind of defeats.

Confines of laws
guarded by instructed snows,
algebraic sand
in the bright green eyes
of charger captives from Kara Koroum.

One must wade across the river
of colorless stag-beetles,
Jolly Rogers
raised on marine roses.

The cloud-lit autumn
—honey of blown glass—
blurs the farewell of the sculptures.
Museums of flesh
delivered to the prism of geometry.

Claw perfume
floating about on the eclipse of lips,
blood scraped from moons
on the granite of returns.

Hands covered with rings are caressing the pink palm trees,
odalisques of sun on the fresh bed of night fire.

Svelte ephebes
are incensing the abyss of the sources of the sky,
on silken carpets
a sword divides the ancient worlds.

Courtesans are abandoning themselves to the sea,
their marble hands are churning up massive drownings.
O you dead of the between-seasons!

Fallow eyes
profane the yellowing grass of strolls,
dried up palace shadows,
rusted enclosures of yawning burns.

Face to face the invasions of rage
buried in flower fur
and the thick velvets of the blood.

In flaring gold chalices,
mangoes, papayas, and guavas await
the thoroughbreds lacquered with conquered dust.

CADAVER CRACKS IN THE LOTUS POND

The sun concludes
in the fountain of tablas,
a lacework of gems bedizened with bones
rusting under the drunken iodine of the idols.

At the call of the lavenders,
doubt encircles the migratory dusks,
serene mutilations before the port.

From Varanasi to Jahangira
a sadhu hypnotizes the Ganges,
a paralysis of flowers and cremation scents
in view of beardless carrion eaters.

The earth slips
between the fangs of the gods,
horns of plenty.

Drowned man,
reopen the wrought anemone gate,
a tentacular blood of lunar ablutions.

In the shadow of a dot,
the third eye reddens,
an acrid almond wandering the snow.

A living cryptogram
of caverns on the flanks of birds
condemned to the frigid vertigo of cascades.

How break this curtain of eyes?
Abandon of a sacrilegious hand
on the pointed phallus of hardened resins.

Cadaver cracks
in the lotus pond,
cries floating the golden lobes.

The volcano has petrified the female incense of a smile,
couplings of millennial entrails
ripened in the tamed silence.

A new hand
lifts the horizon up mane-high.
Ah the galloping of the poles!

Suffering stoops the nettles
deprived of cathedrals,
but who recalls the rugose acanthi
of the zodiac, a forger's leprosy
or a galaxy toll-booth?

Between two eternities
a rutilant garuda encourages
the elephant who has forgotten the forest.

Weighed down under useless gold,
the high priest of images condemns
the snow cult,
a one-eyed skeleton of Cabalistic abortions.

Tortures greedy for sounds,
a herbarium raked by sleep on fire,
under the embers
a rose is devouring the wart hog.
O safari of ejaculatory prayers!

In the nick
of time, the moon, a torque of green harps,
liberates the suave thunderbolt,
a delirium of transparent scarabs.

BIOGRAPHY

In the moldy sea of excavations,
the pollen dissolves the eggs of the sky.

Between the railway walls,
mirrors confuse the rage of clinkers.

Under the rust of stamens,
eyes are hiding behind the vile love of flat swells.

On the drum,
a voice stranded at the edge of a message.

O words shredded
before the out-dated dictionary of hours!

Sinuosities of the blood
snared in the writing of fangs.

Requiems weighed down by toads
blocking the soaring of the veins.

Smiles saturated with flies
on butcher hooks.

In a purulent den,
the newborn child tortures the shadow of the air.

DESTINY

Blood diarrheal
in the bowl of wind,
and in the diary
a child's agony.

ANDEAN HOPES

Writing
riveted to the night-
mare gate.

Skeletons of a soul
littering the mist
where hawsers keep watch.

At the dawn of vows,
the pliability of the snow,
Inti Rami
lays siege to the eyelidless coca.

Schizophrenic,
a snake encircles the mountains,
aborted symbols
of ponderous insubordinations.

Then, in the wing's pit,
the gold of the ascension
peeps through,
a cicatrix chiseled in the penumbra.

DAILY ROUTINE

The sea withdraws
beyond the bundles of cracked eggs,
pavanes of sleep
on the black spume
of sandy carapaces.

A massive upheaval
of premature seconds,
targets too fragile
even for the petrified javelins
of carnivorous flowers.

Enormous turtles
speckled with eyes of fog,
engraving ritual pains
into the mandalas of raucous seaweed.

In revenge,
a one-legged cormorant
—the despot of pubescent isles—
guts
at machine-gun-beak-fire
the pelican swallower of virgins.

A typhoon,
the tourbillion of centuries,
with a grand inner calm,
reposes
on the man-eater lips.

THE FOUR SEASONS OF THE NIGHT

Assassinated fish,
learned assemblies bathed in sweat,
why not imprison
the reflections of sickle forgers?

If the hay butts in,
the stacks have no alternative but to throw up.

In the vomit,
Indians from the north of Mexico
are breeding gamma expansions.

A mushroom questions itself,
in a velvet turgescence,
while the phantoms of Cythera
draw up the soul's anchor.

Crumbling seas cover the wind,
and all the officiants eternalize,
burned by the gall of ophiuroids.

Eclipse of fish-moons
in the celestial shell and in the eye,
a star shard
makes an obscure tear well.

Ah, the four seasons of the night!

THE DISCOVERY

Schizophrenic ants
of the Great Work
penetrating mountains.

Over here,
vibrating, the lanterns
of the isolated on forced march.

Nevertheless, in the black dawn,
we recover the wise fissure
into which dolphins are slipping.

In the crucible,
the eye at last gigantic and alone
for the useless candles.

CALL OF THE CAVERNS

Taper menses, an orgasm
for the blue ants rescued
from an abortive rutting the evening when
the moon hanged itself from snow-
capped pussy sucker tongues.

Inanely happy like a pregnant cloud,
the erect cyclops, his member loaded,
blinds himself with the vaginal oil
that furrows the ovule of worlds.

In an intestinal pocket,
the opium eater unfurls
the sheet of crimson flowers onto the rock-like rumbling
of rejects on the raft
of the Medusa abandoned to
the paralytic calm of crepuscular spasms.

A band of sea urchins praying
in a stone garden penetrate
the mystery of rods, killer
ear wigs lodged
under skull moss,
sepultures of mute musics.

A kleenex wipes
the amplitude of waves, a royal crumple
to dab out the eyes' honey
extractors of chimeres weaned from traitor scorpions.

A river becomes numb,
malicious jelly of grocery witches
sewn at the four fears

of the fair of all men, but the cockroaches,
do they—victims of defective strata—
ignore their executioners?

A necklace of heads, pendulums of the torpor
of subterranean transfusions where sumps
throttle the light, the agony
of a bison—tornado of entrails
and bellowings of stupified hunters—
has revealed the communion
of engravings in the rock's grain.

IMPOTENCE

Just a song facing the red tide
sweeper of pupils, miniatures of chaotic geneses.

But what can music and lyrics do
on the rotting enclosing-wall
of our blind hands,
groping through the foetuses,
a pullulating cannibal people
on the alopecia areata of the sky?

From the bridge, are you keeping watch on
the troubled water,
a mincemeat swarming with scabs,
scrofula in heat
for tender necks?

A man stretched taut
across a crescent moon
begs the invisible archer
to cut his ties to Hades,
to let him follow the arrow of fire.

But on the mirror of the night,
alone,
the faded reflection of a catch-phrase,
vomitings of astrophagous gargoyles.

SECRET ENTABLATURE

A sculpted stone, intense,
listens, decapitated, to
the flexing gears of a Sanskrit saga.

But what use is language when the blood
hides in the clearing.
O vigil of floods of meditations!

Capsizings in dry dock for this bird
without wings, a migrator
within himself, a thirst for invisible voices.

Always, the obsessive moon,
masterless caravan, slow meanderings under eyelids
that loose their leaves onto red trees, absent being.

The annelids dare to dance
and their metameres carry off
the mummies after the vile feast where the sea

choked to death upon returning from the vomitorium.
A chorus beseeches the wind, a gemilliparous germination
in the grain of marble, for the crucified sponges

a phantom apocalypse-triggering smile.

ROYAL HUNT
(First Version)

Behind the wall of vomitings of salamanders arched
against cacti, sadistic flayers of mini-clouds,
puffed up brain cherubs thirsty for a phoenix,
multicolor ashes on a flabby march toward stumbling clocks.

A rattler shakes the charmer, a motionless amulet
on the rock-like rope, file of false dreams,
breakdown of journeys out of breath
in railroad stations husky from insomnia.

A cloud of worms, hairy bird-lime for the harvesting of
syncopated turds, but the air, angel smut,
rolls against the drums at odds with tympanum,
Gothic drunkenness beneath the flamboyants in lotus position;
the storm of a baton on the nape folded against the beat.

Drawn across no snow
the troika makes the stiffened
moulting of the foetal
fractures vibrate.

In the iris, the unicorn's egg, Confucius in a bamboo
half mask, traces on the larvae the tunnel of open
air caves where the mazes become lost, imp inventions
covered with fresh clottings to push back the lightning,
marrowy mirrors where the forger faces of
the triangles are imprinted, altars of repose
for the eye, ah mystery of the shell!

The sphinx—an obsession of cells in which worlds are
    whirling—
absorbs all the formulas, excrement of brainless ants,
and on the lips, runways, the daft smile of Mona Lisa,
a sow escaped from pig bristles.

Self-encirclements, prisons of cuts, scoffing
onslaughts of alphabets without fire, nor letters,
nor wheels, nor women. Ah primitive
flusher of space ships, beaded glass ideograms
where daring hunts etiolate, broken on the strata,
settlings of caverns asphyxiating
the spherical sums of insomniac musics!

DIPTYCH

On the pillowcase,
the sand
of the skeleton dreamer
and the stagnant water of our skin,
a scenery gnawed
by myriads of scolopendras,
water-bugs, blattids, and four-headed cockroaches,
converge
with all the slow sureness of bulldozers
approaching sound-proof mouths.

Nearby,
the fish-water bearer
filters the rectal cadmia
where the star-larvae of warm
mornings nestle
when the sun
pins the butterflies
to hollow orbits.

O the new blossoming of irises!

TO THE CANNIBALS

The bewitchment of a skull
out of which to drink the end of the world
diluted by the thick syrup
of a blood stained
by the globular whites of eyes.

There you wanted to engrave
a relief of stars,
anonymous carcasses
fomenters of miasmas.

In vain the raucous emission
of old moon
swallowing toads,
language has created Babel and Hades.

For want of faith,
the cannibals have resolved nothing,
the last ones would have had
to consume each other!

THE COAL ORCHID

In our empty bladders the vampire winds roar

Swathes of thrashed bat wings
lie in drifts

THE ABSENT FROM THE NIGHT

Leaf eaters
dead under man's breath
unhook
the moon
bullet ridden
by pregnant flies

Into the uteral ponds slide
the pilgrim penises,
tectonic coital thrusts
of emerging darkness

On the vault
the star scales illuminate
the swimming of the signs.

A CAPE OF WILD FLIES

Beyond the silent aurochs-haunted forests,
victims give birth to victims,
white she-wolf jaws crush
the black lord's

epileptic sleigh on the powdery
sand of summer, sand
promised to the horse blood drinkers.
The multiple odyssey under each step!

A hardened rainbow shelters the tarot players
whose fauve oil faces long to crush
the trembling she-mummies
scratching at the surfaceless sheer walls.

Bloodsplashed palettes of eyes.
The fine nerves we entangle in concrete clouds.
After all, the moon does
menstruate on the shadows of our limp

members and bonzai willows dot
the weary fur of our retinas.
Her eyelids hung with deadly nightshade
stuffed bats, her sheets

wet with the blood of virgins,
the royal harpy again and again
yields to peaty crusades of orgasms.
The juice of marine snails

germinated on Uranus streams
from the sex of icy stones
while witches from the Karpaths
anoint the Countess's vaginal chasm.

In the darkness of underground wash houses,
hordes of infuriated, trilobite-fringed
fledglings immerse themselves in the storm graffiti
chiselled in our limestone lungs.

CURDLED SKULLS

The butcher debones the violets
with a suckling's love
for the alpine breast
scattered with curdled skulls

*

At the sprouting of the first bud
a blue shriek of saws
which the madness of the rake would have liked
to twist around its little prongs

*

Sound attacked from every side,
codfish rotting in the beds of bishops
mossy with canonical butts

*

In the flower bed
a slug is urinating on a masochistic spider

*

Obese women with very delicate joints
dragging about bloated snarling cats
packed with porcupine quills

*

Tongues vibrating
in the tops of bald trees
fish shadows teeming
with schools of men

*

Out of breath but smooth with semen
milky spiders
forage in our troubled eyes

*

The bird comes into you through your eyes
ripping out in beakfuls
the tender shoots of your steps

*

Sounds shelled on a rosary of barbed wire

*

In the night of curdled eyes
caterpillars
lay
the droppings of our orphan cries

*

Choked under the mourning caramel
mobs bury themselves
with velvety yells

*

Covered with antique snow
the pollen of our draw-bridge languages

*

Music hanged itself
from a tumefied tongue
in search of an echo
a fly paces up and down

*

An orchestra conductor in tears
elevates to fire's limits
the lacquered veins of luminous winds

*

The sun longs for gravedigging waves
but shivers at the sweet swift swish
of the multicolored harp of razors

*

A capillary breath
marinated in embrace's smut
irrigates
the aurora of the living disguised as the UnDead

END OF THE WALK
(First Version)

To Makiko

Carnival of rusted souls in search of moon
oil to lubricate this eye gear
buried under metallic moss. A note
breaking piano leads, briskly,
this diarrhea of disjointed shadows,
dried up stains where papulous sequins,
the eggs of pythonesses, their breasts
swollen with curdled milk, are teeming.
Their secret desire remains: to sever
the bedbugs, that nibbling mass of tubercular
sun babies, off-springs, soul-orphans
flung to the rocks of oracles,
scrofulous peelings off eyes of glass.
Winds are choking there, a drowning
fanned by the bad breath of goats
defecating mountains of droppings
The Odyssey of Golden Guano.
Do you recall the sirens, those magpie
thieves, free of every cloud? One should
have listened to them; jagged
rocks of the flesh of ecstatic
victims—where can we find you?
Our wobbly incantatory dances raise
a dust of stingings in rut. Ah the titanic
wasp nest engulfer of the shipwreck of
the very last islets of refuge for
tentacle men! Painful contortions for a
mere drop of cervical sap. Bubbles
popping at the inert surface. Nothingness
wandering the deserter void of amnesiac

amnions sabering—to the blows of a scramasax—
a gluey colony of scolopendras, the question mark's
gaseous compositions of jealous gusts.

CURDLED SKULLS

STAINED-GLASS FROST ON PIERS OF MOORED LIPS

their secrets in suspense.

The sun is scuttled into pocket crevices,
locus of the moltings of the void

Strata-encrusted eyes—
solstices weaned of memories
drilled by
fanatics searching for transitory prophecies

A sole cat at
the edge of time
crouches in wait for
ruins.

MIRAMAR

At the edge of its rock
a ghost snaps up foam
immediately dissolved in its shroud.
Below the squalls,
all disappears, only raw heart
drifts
the sand of lost tears

BEZELIK

Ruins raging, jolted by dunes,
drift toward burning blizzards,
dismantlers of the void
perforated by memories.

Sun crumblings
plastered on the raised rejects of the sad earth—
even loyal shadows abandon them.

Where to scoop up some ghastly deceitful
ghost sand in order to recover
our karmic ferrymen
dissolved in an unspeakable alchemy?

PAIN RIPS WATER OUT OF A TORRENT
emerged from a glacial ransom.

Scattered blooming moons thicken
the forever radiated corpse of a shadow.

Smelling of magnets a greenhouse skin
expands the void over the decoys.

Cries crisp the rock-work as soon split by
the hatchet breath of diving bats.

A tin sun laminates tears run wild
that gnomes waylay and nibble.

WINDOWS LOCKED INTO
bony horizons:
the finitude of the soul.

Only the leap
before its time
flings forth the serene sigh of the fall.

Thick word walls clawed
out of praying bowels could not check
the executioner of doubt.

Below, on the concrete,
tepid brown rejected years spread out around
a bland mosaic of looks.

EARTH HOLLOWS OUT IN MY HANDS.
The buzzing of terminal moraines
by a sheer drop of anguish
soldered with sigh-weaned sap.

At the dawn of blood,
already plundered by the outbursts of fate,
between the projections of labial faults,
Artaud's memoir of disjointed planets
blocked by insolent solar barge cats
sweats.

Squatting
between the folding-doors of dusk
a shriek
taunts the fevered horizon of
our pupils slogging on.

AZURE FRACTURES THE ASHEN BLOOD HONEY

suppurating
in voracious bulbs.

The fruitless blooming of a rictus
draped in mist
clawed by hooded crows.

Rocks lie in wait
in mud silence
which vortices squeeze around.

Spiraling eyes struggle in
the breathless drought of flashes.

O demented amnesia of adoption's chaos!

THE SUN STUMBLES AGAINST THE ANCHORED INK.

The page bursts into a fertile mire of continuing eclipses.
Blackness springs back, detoured by tortured shadows.
Eyelids barricade themselves.
Red fury of the unseen
   grave-dredger of memories

SUDDENLY,
in the blood of sublimated sand,
refused skin jams
the clones' gears.

The radial cobwebs of Kafkaesque marathons
emboss with sea teeth
the suspicious aorta of good fortune.

The devil's back:
a helm of cestoidean ice.
How to pave the shadow
under the three sixes?

One,
divisible by the invisible.
Our ashes precipitate
into prophylactic comets.

ZHUANGZI

A bird
alights

on ice.
Its reflection

retains
its flight.

BETWEEN THE SHIFTY PERSPECTIVES
of the depleted fan
flows the fire of chthonian polders
overflowing with oyster-roses.

In a California motel
a hispid penis in blue heat
perfuses the butterfly-swell
of a convulsive wedding.

At the bottom of a labial cave,
lit up by broiling ivory heat,
an unfledged marabou pecks at a third eye
melted in the tepid phosphorescence.

Counterpoint rakes the slow-motion
circles of the serpent thinker's sagittal
dance on transvestite gravel
obsessed with adumbrating moss.

Two camel spiders
weaned of lunar whey
seal the mammilla
curdled under snapping
messengers from ruptured bladders

The waters have broken
O the lull of thighs!

Who will restrain the haughty
solace of turbulent
springheads returning to their sources?

THE SANDS DOZE OFF
in a reflux of marine trances,
held back coital breath warps the fissures
that fuse in the increasing tempo of
vocalizing mutating hoboes.

Between the edges of chronicling shadows
salt-blind cameleers
dredge their absence,
the only guide for our worried anxieties.

When will the cliff and cave engravers return?
Will the avant-garde of their lithic stanzas
dam up the breakers of the human myth?

O the imperialism of the anthropophagi!

"BLINDMEN MAKE LOVE AT NOON"

To René Depestre

Nine meridians later
in caverns pebble-dashed with blisters,
their embryos—knotted with talismans—
hunt—with lashes of umbelliferous cords—
virtue-dry ovals slashed by a pleading Priapus

Coral tree placentas
snap up the clouds of pedagogue ancestors
draped in conch capes
like the yellow princess dead
at the sight of herself and of Jacmel fireflies

Hadriana has seized
the incantations of the arrak transponder
blown down the caudal gorge
that the salty tails
of nappy black chalk dancers rough up

In nights of the vivid fire flakes
of a rumbling negritude
Creole empusas fornicate with a saraband of evil seers,
rock ninjas of King Christophe
eyeing the orifice of the little corporal

And then in Sans Souci palace
roots, lianas and stumps enshrine
the spinning eye of the poet
who perished while cross-breeding clones

O the duplicity of tongues scythed by
chains of white twisters!

FOR TRISTAN TZARA

Tzara is not dead—only pretends to be, and on This
I will once more erect my eclipse.
Tombs remain the best mail slots for our fugues on
that menstrual flood where Moses drifted
between two buoyed nipples
among the reeds of the Pharaoh,
that embalmer of honeymoons and pickled egos.

The moon repeats its palatial belch
transmitting the old hieroscratched code of heliotropic
priests, sullen lickers of baby scarabs.
Quite a few Dada wars ago
a whole new gang of rich Romans attempting
to surpass the frog, trying to grow larger
than the bull's-eye bull, suckled
she-wolf udder and deified the milk.

Dali was wrong to identify the Bible as runny
cholesterol cheese, it was in fact
the dairy Latin Empire, the cultured
rennet of the Pax Romana!

Morning returns to its stoned ignovimous doors
while the ceratorhine Christ
plants his parturient cross of gemellary snakes
in the blessed bowels of chrysopidae.
They cannot be ransomed by scalping ice caps
camouflaged as Artaud's
sawtooth buttocks, especially since
his theatrical double was caught black-handed in
Marat's bath disguised as Charlotte
putting the last touch to her purist royal pear coulis.

In the two-faced mud of shut eyes
the gold fish of the Rising Sun makes lies glitter
but these lies quickly turn as green as withered
angels' wings. A great wall of unicorns
—Confucian messengers?—
rolls and closes in on the belly
invented with each penetration,
and high noon? Encumbered with flies
and weighed down by mythology's malefices,
it thrusts forth its polar bear star, snorkeling under
the very black ice that our orbits furrow.

Albino spiders have confessed their fetid sins to
the shrimp and raucous seabass
dangling from Don Juan's certified neck.
In the Dunhuang caves serene stains of bambini
laced with Ovid syrup
have been raked into a Ryoan-ji
strip of tyrannous
genitals, sighing fire, poached in Tzarist vapor.

Tristan is gone, without even leaving an abbess.
A frieze of lacquered camels
gnawn by pycnogonidic cenobites,
has been beribboned with blighted tapir prayers.
Dragging along the stucco banks of our resentment,
a horde of bearded captains with spongy
eyes are sodomizing buttered flies.

MY HEAD IS ONLY A STONE BUMP,
an old battered millstone with peeling brain—
on its wrinklish hub sleep is crumbling.

The mind confined to its bony cangue
bends toward the icy void of the spirals
of sere moons. Skeletal ages

allow themselves to be carted away
toward nested deltas, muggy shifting mosaics
in which our fractal souls become mired.

Stars, the funerary emblems of mummy hordes,
sponge the overflow from their black holes
where our pendulums come unscrewed.

THE BIRD DIVES INTO MY MOUTH,
explodes, into a forest of sails I fly off.

Cries, chants catch on the warp of leaves,
in this sweating lattice curious hatchings flake.

A viscous light spreads, stirs,
molts into tiny black squamae.

The wind rises over sexes in seisms
to fall squash on serene death.

SECRET CAPITAL

An intense
decapitated
sculpted
stone
listens to the wheelwork
of a Sanskrit saga.

But how can language matter at all
when blood cowers
on the axis of meditation?

Capsizings in dry dock for this wingless bird
migrating to itself, thirsty for the invisible.

The obsessing moon
forces its meanders under
caravans of eyelids bearing red trees
shed of absence.

Annelids dare to dance
and their metameres
drag away the mummies after
an awful banquet during which the sea choked
while returning to the vomitorium.

A choir begs the wind
to make the marble germinate
but a smile alone
launches the apocalypse of spongy crosses.

THE RUN-OUT FROM STONES

slips through the sloping defile
where, stage by stage,
at the edge of an echo's troatings
the sand of the shadows dies.

NAZCA LINES

The sharp nails of the dead
with allotropic skulls scratch the orbits
of condors and of hummingbirds.

The magnetic wind's sand rushes under
the fur of monkeys
forgotten on the altar of shattered cycles.

This epic of traces
hollows out the transparency of abolished towers,
a pilgrimage of indomitable shadows.

The firmament's cicatrixes
offered to the particle ferrymen
close in on the void that time's doubt sifts.

UNIVERSAL SPELEOLOGY

Cathedrals engulfed under cobras
allow the peppery will-o'-the-wisps to escape

Ready to boogie under your eyelids
you'll find tarantulas weaving treacherous transparencies
in which daredevil termites are heaped

Watch out for snapping trunkless heads,
they're on a quest for decayed souls.

With a sulfuric puff the apprentice sorcerer
in the garden of black flowers
crystallizes the harmony in sacred cow-dung
while watching a hill of ants harvesting snow,
a vital spice for that palace of egg layers.

O the princely dervish taste-buds
along the narrow crest of vaginal waves,
whirlwind snatchers of surfer tongues!

So many forgotten basilicas in the genitals of caverns!

Drop down onto your back, mouth open,
to receive from the stalactites, drip by drip,
the thick menstrual loess inundating
The Planet of the Frost-Clawed Bears

RAMAPITHECUS AND CONSORTS

In one man's excavation were found prayers
hammered into dorsal columns
and compressor words in his dried-out brain.

Flies are lying in wait for
the echo of horoscopes across the shaved
pubes of adolescent pythonesses
offering themselves to eagles

You could smash your jaws
against the musical breakwater,
the stolid invention of extraterrestrials,
those absentee assassins of Bolero and consorts.

O the lethal whining of monks in epileptic ecstasy
as they drill into the innermost being
of a choir of throat-slashed seagulls
at the pistil-point of a sweet, irrepressible ascent

Snow-swollen gongs gush from the sweat of bumblebees,
a new unseizable species.
So you become a stupified entomologist
confronting the eddies of their wadded tears.

A woman incarnates it.
Her incarnadine
antipodal grotto closes over you,
the prisoner of liberty.

Death—is it not this unbearable joy
in which is enchased
inaccessible, blown-out mountain ranges
burped out of neurons?

A brick-furred monkey celebrates New Year,
capering through the shade of
the marasmoid kingdom where we lie,
wind troglodytes
inseminated with the solitude of the masses.

Now, when will they start manufacturing angels?

TEMPEST

No respite for the leeches
riveted to our eyes,
pleated, capricious fans
for Art Deco nymphomaniacs
hunting down jungle game giving birth.

We will go bathing our smiles,
lacquered by wings brushing madness over lagoons
heaped with tattered equinoxes.

The carrousel of the dunes whirls
lashing up
the stinging music of rebel sand.

PASSAGE

Foaming rose petals erupt from dark
sea serpents emasculated by firebrand antlers

After a vaporized storm, glassy eyes float about,
burial mounds invading the bolted stars

The sapid trances of space ripple through
our thawing genitalia up into our earwiggy lips

Floccules of silence roost on penises hoisted home

O the narrow galaxy channel through which every little bird
blusters!

MEDITATION

In the ciboria of the towers
are piled our castrated brains,
open wounds quashing the dreams of bats,
mute pilgrims bouncing off karmic wheels

Even the echoes of absence
vanish in the public quicksand,
the secret toll of a solar circus
in which the last robot grapples with gladiators

To monitor the slump of our lice-eaten
tongues we must awaken
the recumbent cyclopes under
the ignorant skins of millennia in labor

Stunned rats will hatch
between the sunset's gums.

LIBERATION

A sudden downdraft of blood mushrooms
imploding in a rose of wind,
carriers of violet deltas in which space floats.

Walleyed walruses absorb,
by the myriads, the black holes
anchored in the eye's void.

The aborted screams of maddened mares
crystallize into icy testes
on which wolf moons bleed to eclipse.

Inside maidenheads bursting with fish yells
a typhonic cloud of crows
pecks away at our candy brains.

ARCHERY

An archer monk draws
tight
the soundless music of an ice
rainbow
that penguins dot
with their solitude.

In the autumn of breath,
the fully-bloomed target
fuses
with the arrow-man.

Bull's-eye:
the trajectory of absence
in the absent
trajectory.

THE HUNT

A bird with nielloed tentacles
grabs the head of a half-breed Christ
anxious to dance the Albatross Calvary
to the barking of flies.

To our dismay
pain cannot redeem our ignorance
nor its rockbound jargon
exorcise Watteau's flowery charnel-parks.

Some sweet-heart of a traitor
lets gangs of asexual jeweled bores
with glued-on hippo smiles
ruin the feast of the circumcised rats
embarked for Cythera.

Faces in flames assault our riverine beds.
Too cool for true rest,
we must ferret out the dream poachers,
stop the fatal loss of our sap.

COPULATIONS

Sulfur meanders flow across
the soft-shelled copulations of hominids.
Glowing with purple sweat they invade
the dilated pupils of the breathless opponents
mollified by shaman semen

Serpents on a pilgrimage to phantoms' hearts
meditate endlessly under the baton of a fistic Bosch

Mirrors tattooed by prenatal game
imprint themselves
on the staring lingams of their kin

At the bottom of the uteri
the microscopic mold of our early babblings
bounces off the Ark's meatus

Miraculous barnacle!

THE ROYAL HUNT
[Second Version]

Salamanders vomit into the sacred
divinatory well
arched against cacti,
deflowerers of obese brains
and thirsty for
multicolored phoenix ashes falling softly
onto clocks cutting open
the hot mists.

A rattlesnake convulses the shaman
swallower of ecstatic flights and fake dreams
on his tightrope strung with amulets
at the edge of a breathing
prosperous with insomnia.

A wormy glue
gives a velvet sheen to the harvest of
syncopated droppings
but the burning angelic air
rolls against the drums in a tympanic
rupture, a gothic intoxication under
the flamboyant rose windows.

Dragged across no snow
a troika makes the rigid molting of fetal
fractures vibrate.

In the iris, the egg of a Confucian unicorn
wearing a black bamboo mask,
a maze of clots has been plotted
so as to mislead Dedalus,
that cunning juggler of creamy mirrors

branding forgers' faces with triangles,
repositories of the Eye—
O the mysteriousness of a shell!

The sphinx surveying the deserted
agora absorbs all the formulaic
excrement of frivolous ants, and
on runway strip lips the simpleton
smile of the Mona Lisa
eludes porcine bristles.

The unphased ego encircles itself with
cuttings of scoffing alphabets
without fire
nor mail
nor wheels
nor woman
—O primate tracker
of space vessels for daring hunts
growing feeble
in the cavernous compression
asphyxiating the spheres,
glass trinkets of narcoleptic musics.

END OF THE WALK
[Second Version]

A carnival of rusted souls files by
in quest of moon oil for
their eye cobwebs buried under metal moss.
A discombobulated shadow piano
enchants the pythonesses' eggs with swollen
quail breasts. Their secret desire
remains to wean grimalkin bed bugs fond of
tubercular sun siblings,
soul orphans
jettisoned to the oracle riff-raff.

The scrapings from eyes bung winds
stoked by goats exuding golden guano.
Do you remember those siren
stealers of magpies, those cloud-clad virgins?
One should have listened to them.

Jagged rocks of ecstatic flesh—
where can we find you again?
Our incantatory dances tamp down
a dust of rutting stingers.
O the titanic wasp nest masticating
the shipwreck of bubble refugees!

Amnesiac amnions desert the void
sabring with scramasax blows
whole colonies of scolopendras
in the gaseous marchlands.

INTRODUCTION
TO SEA URCHIN HARAKIRI

B ernard Bador's poetry to date is surely one of the most unique bodies of work to have been influenced by a range of French poetry that begins with Lautremont, passes through Tzara and the various Surrealist strategies of the 20s and 30s, and, for Bador, culminates in the poetry of St.-John Perse. While Bador acknowledges Perse as his most prominent predecessor, in the poetry of the latter it is as if Perse's galleons of light and renewal are suddenly sucked down into the still, black sheen of a petrified whirlpool. Bernard Bador's poetry evokes faceless lakes of stillbeing, grids of flashing lesions, and a garroted apocalypse resplendent with repugnant urges. There is an appetite for slivers here, a special morbidity that recalls the sensibilities of the German poets Georg Trakl and Gottfried Benn (especially the Benn of the lugubrious and slashing Morgue poems, where one finds such images as mice building a nest in the belly of a little girl whose murdered corpse was left in a ditch).

If such an image were to appear in a Bador poem, even the consistency of natural disintegration would be warped. The mice might be pregnant with flies, and the little girl, still alive (like one of Hans Bellmer's violated waifs), might be watching the mice, gagged with a cross of excrement. Anticipation of natural event in

Bador is always rudely detoured, but at the point that conflicting images start to melt into senselessness, meaning again raises its head, even if wearing its own brain like a perverse tiara.

By locating Bador's writing in a vein that is more Eastern European than French or even German (the world of Vladimir Holan in contrast to that of Paul Eluard), I am actually moving toward the poet's own roots. Bernard Bador is not merely of Hungarian ancestry, but a descendant of the noble Báthory family, which not only included a King of Poland, governors and princes of 16th and 17th century Transylvania, but in those gloomy mountains drained of light from whose folds issued werewolves and mandrakes, the Countess Erzsébet Báthory (1560–1614), a one woman "death camp," who is on record as having hideously tortured and slaughtered over 600 virgins in order to renew her youth by bathing in their blood.[1]

While Bador can hardly be said to have been dominated by a particular ancestor who lived 400 years ago, the coagulated and demonic power in Erzsébet's image appears to have influenced, or flown into, his immediate background so as to affect the nature of his soul, and thus his poetry. I am not one to smirk at the possibility that unappeased, "hungry ghosts" continue to travel the branchings of a family tree until finding a food source, or release, in a particular descendent.

In Bador's poetry at large, and, as I will point out, particularly in his title for this selection, I think it is possible that Erzsébet's seemingly unappeasable hunger for an eroticized mayhem has subsided—as water might in a landscape, leaving the eroded shapes that make up this poetry. Or to put it slightly differently: such hunger has here taken on the form of static, compact stanzas that as their contents are examined begin to resemble plates of cold funereal meats. I can perfectly well imagine Erzsébet's psyche fluttering about these stanzas, nibbling here, sipping there, finding enough death to preoccupy and distract her from what must have seemed to be an endless, ravenous flight through Báthory/Bador progeny.

One reason that I feel this way is that there is no sense of personal experience in Bernard Bador's poetry. The experience is ancestral. Shafts of dusty light reach back to migrations and caravans, to Buddhistic and Hinduistic images, which is to say: a sense of the universe is present. However, it is present as detritus. In contrast to the world of Perse, in which event is always contoured with the rainbow hues of so many stories, in Bador there is incessant entropic closure. Each stanza is an orphan, a little isolated isle, with only possible ties to the one that is found before or behind it. Momentary evocations of grandeur are abruptly double-crossed by torture, disembowelment, and abortion. Reading him is like watching little pieces being broken off from stories and collaged in such a way that omnipotency and impotency are like grooved pipes that screw into each other perfectly.

What makes these poems unique is the way in which they utilize various Surrealist strategies (especially black humor, Objective Hazard, and the estrangement of sensation) without edging in under the canopy of an established Surrealist voice. The extent to which there is any voice at all is questionable. It might be more accurate to say that these are voiceless, breathless poems, poems in which the words do not seem to be uttered, rhythmless words, words more like bric-a-brac or flea market finds. At the same time these words are highly self-conscious of the way they sound. While poems do "open" and "close," the cuts and cauterizations in discrete stanzas are more significant than any thematic development.

The image of sea urchin harakiri, of a sea urchin inflicting death upon itself, using its spines as medieval Japanese samurai ritually disemboweled themselves, has an odd resonance with one of Erzsébet Báthory's most notorious contraptions, her custom-made clockwork Iron Maiden which she herself designed.

By touching the necklace of encrusted stones that ran in a loop down over the chest, the victim set everything in motion. From the interior of the flesh-color painted iron figure would issue the noise of moving clockwork. Arms would raise and embrace whoever was in reach; where the painted breasts were, two shutters slid sideways, the chest opened, and five daggers slowly emerged, stabbing the girl clasped in the embrace. As other gems in the necklace were pressed, the arms fell away and the eyes clicked shut. The girl's blood was collected in a pot and then poured over the Countess who sat upright in an armchair permanently installed in the underground chamber.

Bador's self-inflicting sea urchin image chamber tropes Erzsébet's "virgin press," with the exception, of course, that the image of sea urchin harakiri does not imply a victim other than the sea urchin itself. But if we think of "sea urchin harakiri" as a way of processing images, then the world of the past, the migrations and caravans, etc., become Bador's virgins. What runs into the sea urchin's catchment, or better, what this poet pours over us in a gleeful mockery of his aunt's absurd obsession are "cadaver cracks in the lotus pond," "predatory shipwrecks," "a caterpillar laying the droppings of our orphan cries," as well as "decapitated stones," and "mincemeat swarming with scabs."

Here then is an ample selection, the first to be translated and published in English, of the poetry of Bernard Bador. A Frenchman in his early 40s from Lyon, Bador has lived for over a decade in Los Angeles where nearly all of the poems presented here were written. Since Bador has recently begun to write in English[2], it is quite possible that in the future he will have no need of an American translator.

To make this selection, I have, with Bador's assistance, made a first, literal draft of all of his published poetry (167 poems), as well as over 100 unpublished poems. Based on this initial work, I have completed, on my own, translations of 40 of the 44 poems that make up this book.

Bador's poems in French, more often than not, have only a few words in each line (i.e., he breaks a line where the image "turns," and since thematic possibilities are always being detoured, such "turns" occur frequently). I have found that in English many of the poems come across more forcefully with longer lines, so I have experimented with a number of stanza shapes. I have, however, translated the opening poems in the collection to correspond exactly with the line breaks in the originals.

Several years ago, after meeting Bador in Los Angeles, Robert Kelly wrote the prose poem that the three of us feel is an appropriate gesture with which to end Bernard Bador's American debut.

Clayton Eshleman
Los Angeles, November–December, 1982

[I] All the information here on Countess Erzsébet Báthory comes from Valentine Penrose's *The Bloody Countess*, translated from the French by Alexander Trocchi, Calder & Boyars, London (no date given).

[II] Of the 44 poems in this collection, nearly all are from *Le sang du soleil* (1977), *L'harakiri des oursins* (1980), and *Sphinx asphyxié* (1984), published by Editions Saint-Germain-des-Prés, Paris. "The Coal Orchid," "The Absent From the Night," "A Cape of Wild Flies," and "Curdled Skulls" were edited by the translator from drafts written by Bernard Bador in English. Eight of the poems translated from the French are previously unpublished.

POSTFACE

Prose pour un Lendemain by Robert Kelly

The Countess Erzsébet Báthory (Liz) lived in a language halfway between Hungary and New York. I love her though she was very cruel. She drank the blood of her lovers, and exposed servant girls naked in her snowy courtyard and watched while their robust pinkness turned redder then paler then finally livid. It is interesting that she liked to look at naked women, and that her glance was so dangerous. It hurts people to look at them, the way she and I do. I have been told my eyes burn when I look at people, and I have been likened more than once to a Siberian mink, yes, that's true too, but monk is what I mean, a monk of a later time, one who is still alive, it may be, and singeing dark impressionable gentlewomen with the fervor of his glance. His glance misses nothing. But enough of me. Consider Báthory Erzsébet (as they say in Magyar), Liz, she was a mink too, always at it, sexual to a fault, glossy with desire, a pornosopher-queen, keeping fealty to the lordly impulse that (whether from angel or devil) ran her frantic life. Being in bed with her must have been like being in bed with an orchestra, and not a decorous *hofkapelle* of the time, but a roaring sweating turn of the century magnum of an orchestra, pounding out a Sacre du Printemps or squeezing the last seminal juices from a Verklaerte

Nacht. I think of Liz, in the grip of her wild music, turning her penknives and needles and ice cubes on herself when all other victims were away at church or kept from her by officious major-domos in the pay of her brother the king. I think of her tears of pain and quiver of sheer unfocussed sexuality as drops of blood squeeze out of her pierced thigh; she is just as pink, tender, innocent in the flesh as any of her victims. It makes no difference. She makes the body speak, theirs, her own. She challenges its innocence, challenges its capacity to rouse feeling and be roused. With her lovers she arouses them and herself by the spectacle of wounded girls, wounded boys, and those victims too must have survived or died in some rapt mingling of sensuality and dread half a world's literature has tried to record and decode. The pain of love! Who knew it better than Liz, a Slavic literalist, a Magyar mystic, a catholic metaphorist, a diabolic enthusiast, all her skills to the one question. And that question is a linguistic one, perhaps: what is the word of the body? What is the word of which blood and semen and lymph and vaginal juices are the syllables spelt slowly by the pressure of flesh, at the prodding of steel, cold, heat, wet? I honor her inquiry still: we live in it, we move in it, it seems to be us, seems to carry us wherever there is to go. But what is it, this body, this luscious flesh that time impeaches, *what is it in itself?* Make it speak its name. Like all interrogators, Báthory Erzsébet ultimately relied on torture, *la question*. She too would die under the torturers, and men would fancy that a condign punishment. I think of her dying in orgasm under their screws and rough hempen ropes, the only torture is that her body will speak its word only a moment after she has lost the capacity to hear it, only when she has left the lewd hotel of her flesh and found her naked soul sprawling in the dark of a more than Transylvanian night. Hoofbeats in the wild night, wind, no moon, but some vestigial glow behind the driven cloud wrack, romance, terror and no *au revoir*. Perhaps she stands near us when clumsily we jab needles in our fingers or burn our hands on hot panhandles, or watches us whenever the sexual moment comes. Would we recognize her if, in one of those sudden astral snapshots that whirl through the mind of a lover coming, we suddenly saw a woman we had never seen before, her sculpted lips parted as if to catch word or come? Cold and regal and detached she was painted by the lubricious symbolist Csök Istvan (who moved to Paris and became Etienne Csök), cold in her furs as the poor serving girl is cold in her naked submission to the invisible torture of the weather. That's how they wanted to see things in the Paris salon—all mood and no mayhem—Géricault and all that was well in the angry past. Perhaps the French were right—hold victim and torturer in one careful composition of color and suggestivity, the tension of her burning eyes only to be inferred, and always to be inferred. It is unFrench of me to see so much blood around Liz, and disrespectful thus to the French branch of her family, les Bathory, who in the thumbscrew of time found their name shortened, made more French. My friend Bernard Bador is of that clan, and I speak with him often about his admirable handsome sexy wicked old aunt Liz, *la louve sanglante.*

—Robert Kelly 11/13/80

Poet and artist **BERNARD BADOR** was born in France in 1940. After spending his early years studying the classics, law, political science, Chinese and Russian studies, he moved to Taiwan and spent a number of years in the Far East before moving to Los Angeles. He now resides in Beaujolais but continues to wander, write, and work on his  art on five continents. Bador's collage art has been exhibited on many of those continents. A selection of his art can be seen at www.bernardbador.com.

CLAYTON ESHLEMAN's most recent publications include *The Complete Poetry of César Vallejo*, (University of California Press, 2007), *Archaic Design* (Black Widow Press, 2007), *The Grindstone of Rapport: A Clayton Eshleman Reader* (Black Widow Press, 2008), and *Anticline* (Black Widow Press, 2010). In 2011, Black Widow Press will publish his cotranslation, with Lucas Klein, of Bei Dao's poetry, *Endure*. Also in 2011, Wesleyan University Press will publish his co-translation, with A. James Arnold, of Aimé Césaire's *Solar Throat Slashed*.

TITLES FROM BLACK WIDOW PRESS

TRANSLATION SERIES

Approximate Man and Other Writings
by Tristan Tzara. Translated and edited
by Mary Ann Caws.

Art Poétique by Guillevic.
Translated by Maureen Smith.

Capital of Pain by Paul Eluard.
Translated by Mary Ann Caws, Patricia Terry,
and Nancy Kline.

Chanson Dada: Selected Poems by Tristan Tzara.
Translated with an introduction and essay by
Lee Harwood.

Essential Poems and Writings of Joyce Mansour:
A Bilingual Anthology
Translated with an introduction by
Serge Gavronsky.

Essential Poems and Prose of Jules Laforgue
Translated and edited by Patricia Terry.

Essential Poems and Writings of
Robert Desnos: A Bilingual Anthology
Edited with an introduction and essay
by Mary Ann Caws.

EyeSeas (Les Ziaux) by Raymond Queneau.
Translated with an introduction by Daniela
Hurezanu and Stephen Kessler.

Furor and Mystery & Other Writings
by René Char. Edited and translated by
Mary Ann Caws and Nancy Kline.

The Inventor of Love & Other Writings
by Gherasim Luca. Translated by Julian
and Laura Semilian. Introduction by
Andrei Codrescu. Essay by Petre Răileanu.

La Fontaine's Bawdy by Jean de la Fontaine.
Translated with an introduction by
Norman R. Shapiro.

Last Love Poems of Paul Eluard
Translated with an introduction by
Marilyn Kallet.

Love, Poetry (L'amour la poésie)
by Paul Eluard. Translated with an essay
by Stuart Kendall.

Poems of André Breton: A Bilingual Anthology
Translated with essays by Jean-Pierre
Cauvin and Mary Ann Caws.

Poems of A.O. Barnabooth by Valéry Larbaud.
Translated by Ron Padgett and Bill Zavatsky.

Preversities: A Jacques Prévert Sampler
Translated and edited by Norman R. Shapiro.

The Sea and Other Poems by Guillevic.
Translated by Patricia Terry. Introduction by
Monique Chefdor.

To Speak, to Tell You? Poems by Sabine Sicaud.
Translated by Norman R. Shapiro. Introduction
and notes by Odile Ayral-Clause.

forthcoming translations

Essential Poems and Writings of Pierre Reverdy
Translated by Mary Ann Caws and
Patricia Terry.

I Want No Part in It and Other Writings
by Benjamin Péret. Translated with an
introduction by James Brook.

The Big Game
by Benjamin Péret. Translated with an
introduction by Marilyn Kallet.

A Life of Poems, Poems of a Life
by Anna de Noailles. Translated by
Norman R. Shapiro. Introduction
by Catherine Perry.

MODERN POETRY SERIES

An Alchemist with One Eye on Fire
by Clayton Eshleman

Anticline by Clayton Eshleman

Archaic Design by Clayton Eshleman

Backscatter: New and Selected Poems
by John Olson

The Caveat Onus by Dave Brinks.
The complete cycle, four volumes in one.

Concealments and Caprichos
by Jerome Rothenberg

Crusader-Woman by Ruxandra Cesereanu.
Translated by Adam J. Sorkin. Introduction
by Andrei Codrescu.

Curdled Skulls: Poems of Bernard Bador
Translated by the author with Clayton
Eshleman.

Fire Exit by Robert Kelly

Forgiven Submarine
by Ruxandra Cesereanu and Andrei Codrescu

The Grindstone of Rapport:
A Clayton Eshleman Reader
Forty years of poetry, prose, and translations.

Packing Light: New and Selected Poems
by Marilyn Kallet

Signal from Draco: New and Selected Poems
by Mebane Robertson

forthcoming
modern poetry titles

Endure: Poems by Bei Dao
Translated by Clayton Eshleman and
Lucas Klein

Exile is My Trade: A Habib Tengour Reader
Translated by Pierre Joris.

from stone this running by Heller Levinson

Larynx Galaxy by John Olson

Present Tense of the World: Poems 2000–2008
by Amina Saïd. Translated by Marilyn Hacker.

LITERARY THEORY / BIOGRAPHY SERIES

Revolution of the Mind:
The Life of André Breton
by Mark Polizzotti. Revised
and augmented edition.

WWW.BLACKWIDOWPRESS.COM

This book was set in Adobe Jenson Pro, an old-style serif typeface based on a Venetian typeface cut by Nicolas Jenson in 1470. The cover text was set in Univers, a realist sans-serif typeface designed by Adrian Frutiger in 1954.